W9-ABF-745

e White Fields

7–1980

PR
6027
.O44
W3

# WALKING THE WHITE FIELDS

## Poems 1967–1980

### by Leslie Norris

Salem Academy and College
Gramley Library
Winston-Salem, N.C. 27108

*An Atlantic Monthly Press Book*

Little, Brown and Company     Boston / Toronto

COPYRIGHT © 1970, 1974, 1975, 1976, 1977, 1978, 1979, 1980 by Leslie Norris

All rights reserved. No part of this book may be reproduced in any form or by any electronic or mechanical means including information storage and retrieval systems without permission in writing from the publisher, except by a reviewer who may quote brief passages in a review.

FIRST EDITION

*Acknowledgements*

Some of the poems in "Water Voices" have appeared in *The Anglo-Welsh Review*; *The Atlantic Monthly*; *Delta*; *Limestone*; *The London Magazine*; *The New Statesman*; *The New Yorker* ("Cave Paintings"); *P.E.N. New Poems 1973–1974* and *1976–1977*; *The Poetry Book Society Supplement for Christmas '75*; *Poetry Northwest* ("Ravenna Bridge"); *Poetry Wales*; *The Scotsman*.
*The Yale Literary Magazine* published "Berries" under the title "November Berries."
Thanks are due also to the BBC, ITV, The Globe Playhouse Trust, The South-East Arts Association, Poetry Dimension, and The Tidal Press, Maine.
"At the Sea's Edge, in Pembrokeshire" was commissioned for the 900th-Anniversary Celebrations of Winchester Cathedral.

Norris, Leslie, 1920–
    Walking the white fields.
    "An Atlantic Monthly Press book."
    I. Title.
PR6027.O44W3    821'.914    80-16812
ISBN 0-316-61189-1 (pbk.)

ATLANTIC-LITTLE, BROWN BOOKS
ARE PUBLISHED BY
LITTLE, BROWN AND COMPANY
IN ASSOCIATION WITH
THE ATLANTIC MONTHLY PRESS

MV

*Designed by Janis Capone*

*Published simultaneously in Canada*
*by Little, Brown & Company (Canada) Limited*

PRINTED IN THE UNITED STATES OF AMERICA

*For Robert Manning*

# CONTENTS

## NEW POEMS

# RANSOMS

# CARDIGAN BAY
*(for Kitty)*

The buzzard hung crossed
On the air and we came
Down from the hills under
Him. First sun from
The underworld turned
White his stretched surfaces,
Whitened the cracked stone

On this beach where end
The works of the sea,
The total husbandry
Of water. Now at noon
We walk the land between
The seamarks, knowing

That wave already made
To wash away our happy
Loitering before
We turn back into evening
Among the frail daffodils
Growing in other seasons.

For those who live here
After our daylight, I
Could wish us to look
Out of the darkness
We have become, teaching
Them happiness, a true love.

# WATER

On hot summer mornings my aunt set glasses
On a low wall outside the farmhouse,
With some jugs of cold water.
I would sit in the dark hall, or
                    Behind the dairy window,
Waiting for children to come from the town.

They came in small groups, serious, steady,
And I could see them, black in the heat,
Long before they turned in at our gate
To march up the soft, dirt road.
                    They would stand by the wall,
Drinking water with an engrossed thirst. The dog

Did not bother them, knowing them responsible
Travellers. They held in quiet hands their bags
Of jam sandwiches, and bottles of yellow fizz.
Sometimes they waved a gratitude to the house,
                    But they never looked at us.
Their eyes were full of the mountain, lifting

Their measuring faces above our long hedge.
When they had gone I would climb the wall,
Looking for them among the thin sheep runs.
Their heads were a resolute darkness among ferns,
                    They climbed with unsteady certainty.
I wondered what it was they knew the mountain had.

They would pass the last house, Lambert's, where
A violent gander, too old by many a Christmas,
Blared evil warning from his bitten moor.
Then it was open world, too high and clear
                    For clouds even, where over heather
The free hare cleanly ran, and the summer sheep.

I knew this; and I knew all summer long
Those visionary gangs passed through our lanes,

Coming down at evening, their arms full
Of cowslips, moondaisies, whinberries, nuts,
      All fruits of the sliding seasons,
And the enormous experience of the mountain

That I who loved it did not understand.
In the summer, dust filled our winter ruts
With a level softness, and children walked
At evening through golden curtains scuffed
      From the road by their trailing feet.
They would drink tiredly at our wall, talking

Softly, leaning, their sleepy faces warm for home.
We would see them murmur slowly through our stiff
Gate, their shy heads gilded by the last sun.
One by one we would gather up the used jugs,
      The glasses. We would pour away
A little water. It would lie on the thick dust, gleaming.

# RANSOMS
*(for Edward Thomas)*

What the white ransoms did was to wipe away
The dry irritation of a journey half across
England. In the warm tiredness of dusk they lay
Like moonlight fallen clean onto the grass,

And I could not pass them. I wound
Down the window for them and for the still
Falling dark to come in as they would,
And then remembered that this was your hill,

Your precipitous beeches, your wild garlic.
I thought of you walking up from your house
And your heartbreaking garden, melancholy
Anger sending you into this kinder darkness,

And the shining ransoms bathing the path
With pure moonlight. I have my small despair
And would not want your sadness; your truth,
Your tragic honesty, are what I know you for.

I think of a low house upon a hill,
Its door closed now even to the hushing wind
The tall grass bends to, and all the while
The far-off salmon river without sound

Runs on below; but if this vision should
Be yours or mine I do not know. Pungent
And clean the smell of ransoms from the wood,
And I am refreshed. It was not my intent

To stop on a solitary road, the night colder,
Talking to a dead man, fifty years dead,

But as I flick the key, hear the engine purr,
Drive slowly down the hill, I'm comforted.


The white, star-shaped flowers of the wood garlic, *Allium ursinum*, are usually known as ramsons; but W. Keble Martin, in *The Concise British Flora in Colour* (Ebury Press and Michael Joseph, 1965), calls them ransoms. They grow profusely from April to June in the beech hangers above Edward Thomas's house outside Petersfield. Obviously, in the context of the poem, ransoms means much more than the usual name.

# NOW THE HOUSE SLEEPS

Now the house sleeps among its trees,
Those charcoal scratches on the sky's
Good morning, and I walk the lane
That all night long has quietly gone
Down the cold hill, and quietly up
Until it reached that darkened top
Where the shrill light of a short day
Begins again the frozen glow

Of winter dawn. I contemplate
The wealth of day that has to wait
The recognition of my eye.
Reality is what we see,
Or what my senses all achieve;
What they believe, so I believe.
Around, the ring of hills wears light
Of morning like a steel helmet

And below them, in the brown
Cleansing of its floods, runs down
The brawling river. Now the owl,
That all night held its floating call
Over the terrified hedges, climbs
In clumsy blindness to the elm's
Black safety, there flops down,
A comfortable, daylight clown;

And little animals of night
Retire as silent as the light
To sleeping darkness. Closing the door,
I leave the white fields desert for
The loss of my descriptive eye.
The sunlit measures of the day
Are unregarded. I cut bread,
Knowing the world untenanted.

And yet, although my sight must stop
At the solid wall, a world builds up,
Feature by feature, root by root,
The soft advance of fields, daylight
Reaching west in the turn of life,
Personal, created world, half
Ignorant, half understood. And I
Complete from faulty memory

And partial complexities of sense
Those images of experience
That make approximate rivers move
Through the wrong world in which I live,
Or chart a neat uncertainty
Down major roads to Nowhere City;
But at the edge of what I know
The massed, appalling forests grow.

Through the long night the rough trucks grind
The highways, gears ripping blind,
Headlights awash on the tarmac;
All night long metallic traffic,
Racks of concrete, rams of girders,
Heavy oppression of cities
Forced by a crude growling. Yet all
Are Plato's shadows on the wall,

Noises drifting among shadows,
Shadows dying among echoes,
While clear eternities of light
Shine somewhere on the perfect world
We cannot know. My shadowed field
Lies in its flawed morning, and dirt
Falls in the slow ditches. Sunrise,
And the house wakes among its trees.

# POSTCARDS FROM WALES

Whenever I think of Wales, I hear the voices
Of children calling, and the world shrinks to the span
Of a dozen hills. As I wander to sleep
The water voices of the streams begin.

> *Green air, the truthful winds shall sing you*
> *Over the lean hill and the melancholy*
> *Valley of childhood.*

We swam free rivers that our tongues resembled,
We lit the summer dark with lazy fire
At the waterside. And when silence fell
It was not passing time we grew to hear,

> *Winter. The blind lake turns its solid*
> *Eye to the snowcloud. In the village*
> *The doors are fast, the chimneys fat with coalsmoke*

But the world changing, the tall hills tumbling,
The universe of terraces waning small.
Beyond brief rivers we heard the urgent sea
Knock to come in. It was a miracle

> *The spent salmon drops tail first to the sea.*
> *His lank sides heave. His exhausted eye*
> *Turns away for another year.*

Of our own discovering. Whenever I think of Wales,
I think of my leaving, the farewell valleys letting go
And the quick voices falling far behind in the dust
Off the dry tips. And I think of returning, too,

> *Cae Gwair is spotted with orchises;*
> *The earth, finding its own rich heat,*
> *Releases it in little purple columns.*

On some afternoon warm and loving, to a handful
Of fields by Teifi river and a cottage blind
With waiting. I know those rough, wind-turning
Walls were made in childhood, I know my mind

*In September the cold ponies*
*Return from the high moor. They kick*
*Down the tottering stones and relish the gardens.*

Invents the long, immaculate weather of a year
Unpredictable as truth. But the river's voice
Is forever filling the valley, filling it,
And remembered voices are underneath my windows.

Salem Academy and College
Gramley Library
Winston-Salem, N.C. 27108

# EARLY FROST

We were warned about frost, yet all day the summer
Has wavered its heat above the empty stubble. Late
Bees hung their blunt weight,
Plump drops between those simplest wings, their leisure
An ignorance of frost.
My mind is full of the images of summer
And a liquid curlew calls from alps of air;

But the frost has come. Already under trees
Pockets of summer are dying, wide paths
Of the cold glow clean through the stricken thickets
And again I feel on my cheek the cut of winters
Dead. Once I awoke in a dark beyond moths
To a world still with freezing,
Hearing my father go to the yard for his ponies,

His hands full of frostnails to point their sliding
To a safe haul. I went to school,
Socks pulled over shoes for the streets' clear glass,
The early shops cautious, the tall
Classroom windows engraved by winter's chisel,
Fern, feather and flower that would not let the pale
Day through. We wrote in a cold fever for the morning

Play. Then boys in the exulting yard, ringing
Boots hard on winter, slapped with their polishing
Caps the arrows of their gliding, in steaming lines
Ran till they launched one by one
On the skills of ice their frail balance,
Sliding through life with not a fall in mind,
Their voices crying freely through such shouting

As the cold divided. I slid in the depth
Of the season till the swung bell sang us in.
Now insidious frost, its parched grains rubbing

At crannies, moved on our skin.
Our fingers died. Not the warmth
Of all my eight wide summers could keep me smiling.
The circle of the popping stove fell still

And we were early sped through the hurrying dark.
I ran through the bitterness on legs
That might have been brittle, my breath
Solid, grasping at stabs of bleak
Pain to gasp on. Winter branched in me, ice cracked
In my bleeding. When I fell through the teeth
Of the cold at my haven door I could not see

For locked tears, I could not feel the spent
Plenty of flames banked at the range,
Nor my father's hands as they roughed the blue
Of my knees. But I knew what he meant
With the love of his rueful laugh, and my true
World unfroze in a flood of happy crying,
As hot on my cheek as the sting of this present

Frost. I have stood too long in the orderly
Cold of the garden. I would not have again the death
Of that day come unasked as the comfortless dusk
Past the stakes of my fences. Yet these are my
Ghosts, they do not need to ask
For housing when the early frost comes down.
I take them in, all, to the settled warmth.

# STONES

On the flat of the earth lie
Stones, their eyes turned
To earth's centre, always.
If you throw them they fly
Grudgingly, measuring your arm's
Weak curve before homing
To a place they know.

Digging, we may jostle
Stones with our thin tines
Into stumbling activity.
Small ones move most.
When we turn from them
They grumble to a still place.
It can take a month to grate

That one inch. Watch how stones
Clutter together on hills
And beaches, settling heavily
In unremarkable patterns.
A single stone can vanish
In a black night, making
Someone bury it in water.

We can polish some;
Onyx, perhaps, chalcedony,
Jasper and quartzite from
The edges of hard land.
But we do not alter them.
Once in a million years
Their stone hearts lurch.

# MERMAN
*(for Kit Barker)*

When I first came to the air I fell
Through its empty thickets. Dry
Land attacked me, and I lay
With my skin in grit, drily.
The drab, sudden weight of my
Gagging flesh dragged me, would pull

Me down. Nor would my swimming
Bones erect me. It was a grunting
Crawl I moved at. There was not need
For the rough cords they locked me in.
Later, in the animal compound, pooled
In a small dead water of their making,

I hid my staring sex, and wept.
As my stale gills crumbled
Like bread, and slow lungs held
Air with a regular comfort,
I learned to prod locked bones
To a jolt of walking. Their sounds

Came last to my mouth
And were useful for freedom.
I who had been a sad monster
In the kept zoo of their fear
Live at equal liberty with
Them now. At dark I come

From watching the tame harbour
Where nudged ships depart,
And in my tideless cell I dream
The great seas break far over me,
Silent; and I dream I drift
In upright sea-growth, in the living water.

# A GIRL'S SONG

Early one morning
As I went out walking
I saw the young sailor
Go fresh through the fields.
His eye was as blue as
The sky up above us
And clean was his skin
As the colour of shells.

O where are you going,
Young sailor, so early?
And may I come with you
A step as you go?
He looked with his eye
And I saw the deep sea-tombs,
He opened his mouth
And I heard the sea roar.

And limp on his head
Lay his hair green as sea-grass
And scrubbed were his bones
By the inching of sand.
The long tides enfolded
The lines of his body
And slow corals grow
At the stretch of his hand.

I look from my window
In the first light of morning
And I look from my door
At the dark of the day,
But all that I see are
The fields flat and empty
And the black road run down
To Cardigan town.

# FISHING THE TEIFI

Left bank and right,
I've fished this water since first light,
Pitching my early spinners
Into the river's mirrors,
Feeling the hook sink
Minutely, then I'd check, and bring it to the bank.

It was enough at first
To know the thrown perfection of each cast,
My eight-foot, fibre glass flinger
Growing from my hand, a finger
To set exactly down
My teal and black, mallard and claret, or coachman.

But I've had nothing on
All morning nor the longer afternoon.
For all his hunched attention
The empty heron's flown,
And now the soft-whistling otter
Glides his long belly into the blackening water.

From the bleak dark the hiss
Of a harsh wind turns my face
Down like a sheet, telling me to go.
But sleep tonight I know
Will not shut out this river, nor the gleam
Of big fish, sliding up to hook onto my dream.

# THE ONE LEAF

An oak leaf fell from the tree
Into my hand almost, so I kept it.
First in my fingers, very carefully,
Because it was mine. I wiped it,
Put it on my desk, near the typewriter.
Last autumn there were oak leaves falling everywhere.

I could have chosen from so many.
It lay there months, turning browner,
Before I no longer saw it. Now
Here it is again, an old letter
From plenty. From where I stand
This is the one leaf, in the cold house, on the cold ground.

# IT'S SOMEBODY'S BIRTHDAY

This birthday man
Rises from my hot bed
Into his mirror.
When I groan
Out of his crumpled head
He prods my dewlap with a jeering finger.

Behind his eyes
Lie the slim silver boys
Called by my name.
No blind surprise
Nor moving without noise
Shall ever startle them inside that frame.

To my round skin
He will remain flat true,
Warning for warning.
I pull my stomach in,
March a hard step or two,
Shut loud the bathroom door, murder his morning.

# DRUMMER EVANS

There was a great elm in Drummer Evans's garden.
Half of his house it kept in daylight shadow; all summer
A chaffinch sang in its highest branches, swinging
In an invisible cage its music was so local.
Drummer dribbled it crumbs from his fingers
As he sat on a log, his back to the elm trunk,
One slow leg straight before him, and his yellow hand,
His fingers, playing intricate patterns on his other knee.
He was small, his eyes looked upward always.
His face was mild and ivory, composed and smooth.
He wore a black suit and a very wide hat and he called
All women Mrs. Jones, because it was easier.
I went to him Tuesdays and Saturdays for lessons.

My kettledrum set on its three-legged stand,
He would flick its resonance with a finger and say,
"Now boy, two with each hand, away you go; and
Don't let the drumstick tamp." Tamp was a word for bounce,
We always used it. Away I'd go, two with each hand,
Back of the wrists to the skin, sticks held lightly,
And clumsily double beat with each hack fist,
Tap-tap, tap-tap, tap-tap, until that unskilled knock
Snarled in my tired arms and stuttered out.
I don't remember getting any better, but he'd nod,
Still for a while his drumming hand, and smile,
And say, "Again." When I could play no more he'd take the sticks
And give to my stubborn drum a pliant eloquence.
I'd leave then. The bird was nearly always singing.
It never rained in Drummer Evans's garden.

Because I knew that I would never make
On an echoing hull those perfect measures
Heard in my head as I marched at the head of armies

Or rattling between the beat of my running heels,
I left the Drummer.
                    It was an idle sun
Recalled his garden, and an unclaimed bird
Singing from a thorn his tame bird's song
That brought the old man back,
Martial hands parading and muttering.
I went by the river's edge and stone bridge
To his thundering cottage.

For the air for half a mile was rhythmical thunder.
Roll after roll of exact, reverberant challenge,
The flames of history unfurled their names from my books,
Agincourt, Malplaquet, Waterloo, Corunna,
And I reached at a gasp the Drummer's beleaguered garden.

Ringed by standing friends at the rim of his anger,
He stood strapped for war from the fury of their kindness,
Striking his sharp refusal of all pity
The women offered. "Come on," they called, "Ah, come on Mr. Evans."
But he swept them away with the glory of his drumfire,
Hands flying high in volleys of retaliation.
The tree held its sunlight like a flag of honour
And helpless, uniformed men spoke out to him softly;
But his side-drum returned defiance for this old man
Whose proud skill told us he was Drummer Evans,
No common mister to be hauled to the Poorhouse.

# WINTER SONG

Over the bluff hills
At the day's end
The diffident snow
Swirls before dropping

Blow wind, blow
That we may see
Your smooth body

The humble snow
Is waiting for darkness
So its soft light
Can muffle the hills

Blow wind, blow
The copse will be silent
The black trees empty

At the day's end
The small snow is scurrying
White bees in the moon
And the flying wind

Blow wind
Over the cold hills
For the moon is voiceless

# GRASS

I walk on grass more often
Than most men. Something in me
Still values wealth as a wide field
With blades locked close enough
To keep soil out of mind. It is a test
Of grass when I push a foot
Hard on its green spring. The high pastures
I mean, open to the unfenced wind,
Bitten by sheep.
                Go into Hereford,
My grandfather said (his dwarf
Grass was scarce as emeralds,
The wet peat crept brown into his happiness),
In Hereford the grass is up to your waist.
We could not gather such unthinkable richness,
We stared over the scraped hill to luscious England.

Behind us the spun brook whitened
On boulders, and rolled, a slow thread
On the eyes, to bubbling pebbles.

I have been in wet grass up to the waist,
In loaded summer, on heavy summer mornings,
And when I came away my clothes, my shoes,
My hair even, were full of hard seeds
Of abundant grass. Brushes would not remove them.

Winters, I know grass is alive
In quiet ditches, in moist, secret places
Warmed by the two-hour sun. And as the year
Turns gently for more light,
Viridian grass moves out to lie in circles,
Live wreaths for the dying winter.

Soon roots of couch-grass,
Sly, white, exploratory, will lie
Bare to my spade. Smooth and pliable,
Their sleek heads harder
And more durable than granite.
It is worth fighting against grass.

# THREE MEN

### 1. Billy Price

He would open the loft early
And his soft-voiced flock
Turned in the morning
Like a bird with a hundred wings.

On workless days he would sing
Freely, and girls in neighbouring
Backyards applauded him
With joined choruses and the frankness of their smiles.

At evening he would signal in his pigeons.
When I began to whistle I learned this call;
A ladder of falling notes across the bars as the birds
Folded themselves home.

### 2. Harry the Black

We spent our boyhoods throwing him insults
And stones, but they bounced off his round dignity.
Later we spoke to him with careful, adolescent seriousness
While our friends tied "Little Demons" to his coattails.

He leaped through the Police Station doorway
Yelling "Jesus!" at every explosion.
His face was Jamaican black.
We avoided him if we were alone.

One of the Dowlais boys, home from the Irish Guards,
Brought with him an exotic Chinese wife.
Harry was appalled. "Foreigners," he said,
"Bloody foreigners in our country!"

## 3. John Williams

His father had drunk away many acres
And a whole flock of mountain sheep.
He had been tall, red-bearded, strong as legend,
Ridden to market on a pony much too small,

But John Williams was deliberately not like this.
Mild and silver from his youth,
He had refused even to grow very much.
At fourteen I was inches over his eighty years.

The day he was eighty we leaned on his gate
And he told me of his fading eyes.
There was a signpost on the horizon opposite
He could scarcely see. Staring at that far

Mountain-edge, I could see only the dissolving
Motes of the air. But he had turned away.
"When you are old," he said, "when you are old
You know where all the fingerposts are."

# DOG

On a field like a green roof
Pitched by the sea-wind
A patch of uncertain sheep
Each poised on pointed hoof
Ready for running
Stare at the coiled bitch
Alert for their turning

And stamp as she sidles
And freezes. They pick
At the steep field, they back,
Disturbing the nervous edge
Of their fleecy circle.
Slowly the bitch inches
And with a rush

Channels the stunned run.
They stream in a prim file
Through the one marked gap
In the leaning hedge,
And Fan, tongue sideways lolling,
Ushers them softly through.
Adrift on the stiff hill

The cold shepherd does not even watch them.

# SPACE MINER
*(for Robert Morgan)*

His face was a map of traces where veins
Had exploded bleeding in atmospheres too
Frail to hold that life, and scar tissue
Hung soft as pads where his cheekbones shone
Under the skin when he was young.
He had worked deep seams where encrusted ore,
Too tight for his diamond drill, had ripped
Strips from his flesh. Dust from a thousand metals
Silted his lungs and softened the strength
Of his muscles. He had worked the treasuries
Of many near stars, but now he stood on the moving
Pavement reserved for cripples who had served well.
The joints of his hands were dry and useless
Under the cold gloves issued by the government.

Before they brought his sleep in a little capsule
He would look through the hospital window
At the ships of young men bursting into space.
For this to happen he had worked till his body broke.
Now they flew to the farthest worlds in the universe:
Mars, Eldorado, Mercury, Earth, Saturn.

# THE DEAD
*(after the Welsh of Gwenallt, 1899–1969)*

Reaching fifty, a man has time to recognise
His ordinary humanity, the common echoes
In his own voice. And I think with compassion
Of the graves of friends who died. When I was young,

Riding the summer on a bike from the scrapyard,
Kicking Wales to victory with all I could afford —
A pig's bladder — how could I have known
That two of my friends would suffer the torn

Agony of slimy death from a rotten lung,
Red spittle letting their weakening
Living into a bucket? They were our neighbours,
Lived next door. We called them the Martyrs

Because they came from Merthyr Tydfil, that
Town of furnaces. Whenever I thought
I'd laugh, a cough ripped over the wall,
Scraping my ribs with cinders. It was all

Done at last, and I crept in to look,
Over the coffin's edge and the black
Rim of the Bible, at the dry flesh free
Of breath, too young for the cemetery.

And I protest at such death without dignity,
Death brutally invoked, death from the factory,
Immature death, blind death, death which mourning
Does not comfort, without tears. I bring

From my mind a small house huge with death,
Where heavy women cut sticks, deal with
The fires, the laborious garden, their little
Money dissolving in the hand. Terrible

Are the blasphemous wars and savageries I
Have lived through, animal cruelty
Loose like a flame through the whole world;
Yet here on Flower Sunday, in a soiled

Acre of graves, I lay down my gasping roses
And lilies pale as ice as one who knows
Nothing certain, nothing; unless it is
My own small place and people, agony and sacrifice.

# OWLS

The owls are flying. From hedge to hedge
Their deep-mouthed voices call the fields
Of England, stretching north and north,
To a sibilant hunt above ditches;
And small crawlers, bent in crevices, yield
Juice of their threaded veins, with

A small kernel of bones. It was earlier
I walked the lace of the sea at this south
Edge, walked froths of the fallen moon
Bare-legged in the autumn water
So cold it set my feet like stones
In its inches, and I feel on breath

And ankles the touch of the charged sea
Since. I saw in my lifting eyes the flat
Of this one country, north stretching,
And north. I saw its hills, the public light
Of its cities, and every blatant tree
Burning, with assembled autumn burning.

I know the same sun, in a turn
Of earth, will bring morning, grey
As gulls or mice to us. And I know
In my troubled night the owls fly
Over us, wings wide as England,
And their voices will never go away.

# OCTOBER IN THE LANE

October in the lane, and the thin harebells,
Ghosts of their deep Augusts, pine in the hedges.
Puffed leaves thicken the crawling ditches
And tired wasps labour in the air,

Heavy with dying. Our trees prepare
The black calligraphies of winter, we strip
Our fields for the frost fire. Now roses drop
From the wall their falls of petals

And cheat my eyes with snowflakes. Smells
Of marauding weather come coldly in with the dark.
I remember a spring of snow that fell without mark
On my head and white hurry as I thudded for home

And we laughed to see how soon I became,
In a falling minute, a seven-year-old, white-haired man.
In the kitchen mirror I watched the quick years run
From the warm, and I wiped from my head

the unready white my April time pretended.
So many weathers have spread their tempers near me
That empty winters stretch behind my mirror
And the keenest razor will not shift their snowfalls.

# OLD VOICES

First the one bell, heavy, behind it
Centuries of controlled certainty, swung
With an enormous sound past
The kneeling city; it is the first
Heard stone in an architecture of ringing.
And sung in at built intervals, at
The joint of locked structure, the voice
Of the second bell. The foundation is

Set on unimpeded air. An age
Of cut stone and iron — those old
Technologies — has its immense medieval
Tongues bellowing again. Now all
The small bells filigree and stretch
A long nave in the ear and a pulled
Spire of sailing clamour. Resonant
Cathedrals of listening are launched

On the open day. But bells are not
Peaceful; are arrogant with the complete
World of their origin. Think, imagine,
In the clack of swords they began,
Short on their own shields the flat beat
Struck, so that erratic courage set
Hard in the metal; then the high edge,
Turning in the urgency of the charge,

Rang through the heads of wives
At their keen mourning. Hacking the bent
Angles of helmets, rough blades cracked again
The wombs that bore these splintered heads
In their early down. From such sounds,
From the held quiet after, the brazen
Complexities of the loud tower grew.
There was time for the patterns of victory,

And space on the fat plains of grain
For building of flawless bells. The lost
In their slate hills had tongues only,
Grew old in the slow labour
Of changing myths. Through the mist
Of altering voices their stories spun,
Through generations of telling. Spiral
Images from the belfries, the metal

Confections of chiming, are not
For the mountains. Old men tell
Of an impermanent peace, a fragile
Faith is passed through narrative
Villages in syllables of live
Whispers. Foolish now to regret
Centuries of locked exile. It happened.
We have heads full of easy legend

And elegies like the cold sun
Of treeless autumn. I carry
Such tunes in my head like the thin
Silence the bells hang in. But from
These reaching fields my surnamed
Fathers came, the great cathedrals
Counted them. I walk their lanes,
My shoes cover the concave stones

Worn by their slow tolling.
If I speak with the quick brooks
Of the permanent hills, in my saying
See hordes of the dark tribes stand,
Their faces hidden, my hand
In its perfect glove of skin holds
Other ghosts. We step the streets
Uneasily, disturbed by bells.

# A TRUE DEATH
*(for Vernon Watkins, 1906–1967)*


When summer is dead, when evening
October is dying, the pendulum
Heart falters, and the firm
Blood hangs its drops in a swing
Of stone. Laughing, we catch breath
Again. But his was the true death

Our rehearsals imitate. I lived
On the charred hills where industrial
Fires for a hundred years had grieved
All things growing. On still,
On the stillest days, a burnish
Of sea glinted at the world's edge

And died with the sun. There
Were twenty miles of Wales between
My streams and the water lore
He knew. He watched the green
Passages of the sea, how it rides
The changing, unchanging roads

Of its hollowing power. Caves
From his flooded cliffs called to him,
Dunes with their harsh grasses
Sang, the river-mouths spoke of home
In Carmarthen hills. Small stones
Rang like bells, touching his hands.

Last year we sat in his garden,
Quietly, in new wooden chairs,
Grasshoppers rasped on the hot lawn.
Shadows gathered at his shoulders
As he spoke of the little tormentil,
Tenacious flower; growing there still.

# MOUNTAINS POLECATS
## PHEASANTS
## AND OTHER ELEGIES

# STONE AND FERN

It is not that the sea-lanes
Are too long, nor that I am not
Tempted by the birds' sightless

Roads, but that I have listened
Always to the voice of the stone,
Saying: Sit still, answer, say

Who you are. And I have answered
Always with the rooted fern,
Saying: We are the dying seed.

# BARN OWL

Ernie Morgan found him, a small
Fur mitten inexplicably upright,
And hissing like a treble kettle
Beneath the tree he'd fallen from.
His bright eye frightened Ernie,
Who popped a rusty bucket over him
And ran for us. We kept him
In a backyard shed, perched
On the rung of a broken deck-chair,
Its canvas faded to his down's biscuit.
Men from the pits, their own childhood
Spent waste in the crippling earth,
Held him gently, brought him mice
From the wealth of our riddled tenements,
Saw that we understood his tenderness,
His tiny body under its puffed quilt,
Then left us alone. We called him Snowy.

He was never clumsy. He flew
From the first like a skilled moth,
Sifting the air with feathers,
Floating it softly to the place he wanted.
At dusk he'd stir, preen, stand
At the window-ledge, fly. It was
A catching of the heart to see him go.
Six months we kept him, saw him
Grow beautiful in a way each thought
His own knowledge. One afternoon, home
With pretended illness, I watched him
Leave. It was daylight. He lifted slowly

Over the Hughes's roof, his cream face calm,
And never came back. I saw this;
And tell it for the first time,
Having wanted to keep his mystery.

And would not say it now, but that
This morning, walking in Slindon woods
Before the sun, I found a barn owl
Dead in the rusty bracken.
He was not clumsy in his death,
His wings folded decently to him,
His plumes, unruffled orange,
Bore flawlessly their delicate patterning.
With a stick I turned him, not
Wishing to touch his feathery stiffness.
There was neither blood nor wound on him,
But for the savaged foot a scavenger
Had ripped. I saw the sinews.
I could have skewered them out
Like a common fowl's. Moving away
I was oppressed by him, thinking
Confusedly that down the generations
Of air this death was Snowy's
Emblematic messenger, that I should know
The meaning of it, the dead barn owl.

# AT USK

On a cold day, in the church-
yard, between the gate and
the west door's unlocked arch,

lay the flat stone. It was
anonymous. It might have
gained by chance its grace

of simple effigy, round
eyeless head, rough torso,
a hint of sleeping child

in its stillness; a brown
stone of Monmouthshire
shaped and polished by rain.

A child was kneeling there,
absorbed, concentrating,
measuring with happy care

on the cold of breast
and throat her offering
of snowdrop and crocus.

She matched the flowers,
placed them on the stone
child with her red fingers,

and then ran off to some
warm house in the town.
Now on the stone a film

of winter sap sticks the
limp stalks, but it is
the child at home that I

think of as I walk quickly
through God's still acre.
Her gifts delight me, and I

am leaving Usk, moving
toward the M4, clearly
right to praise the living.

# A GLASS WINDOW,
# IN MEMORY OF EDWARD THOMAS,
# AT EASTBURY CHURCH

The road lay in moistening valleys, lanes
Awash with evening, expensive racehorses
Put to bed in pastures under the elms.
I was disappointed. Something in me turns

Urchin at so much formality, such pastoral
Harmony. I grumble for rock outcrops,
In filed, rasping country. The church drips
Gently, in perfect English, and we all

Troop in, see the lit window, smile, and look
Again; shake out wet coats. Under your name
The images of village, hill and home,
And crystal England stands against the dark.

The path cut in the pane most worries me,
Coming from nowhere, moving into nowhere.
Is it the road to the land no traveller
Tells of? I turn away, knowing it is, for me,

That sullen lane leading you out of sight,
In darkening France, the road taken.
Suddenly I feel the known world shaken
By gunfire, by glass breaking. In comes the night.

# HIS LAST AUTUMN
*(for Andrew Young, 1885–1971)*


He had never known such an autumn.
At his slow feet were apples
Redder than sun, and small flowers,
Their names no longer thought of,

Grew afresh in his recovered innocence.
His eyes had taken colour of the speedwell.
Looking at the sea, he felt its
Lifting pull as he dived, years deep,

Where slant light picked the rocks
With brilliants. It was the distant
Road of his boyhood we drove along
On sunny afternoons, it was the laid

Dust of his past that rose beneath
Our wheels. Tranquilly the weather
Lingered, warm day after warm day.
He was dead when the cold weather came.

## THE YEW TREE ABOVE THE GRAVE OF
## DAFYDD AP GWILYM

*(after the Welsh of Gruffudd Gryg, fl. 1360–1400)*

A tree grows at the wall
Of Ystrad Fflur, the great hall.
God's grace to it, for it is blessed
To be the house of Dafydd,
And his own spent beauty
Dafydd gives to the yew tree.

Even before you grew
Dafydd said this of you:
You were named for his home,
Death's keep against storm,
Against blizzard, hard wind;
As once birches were kind
In the snows of his manhood.
Now he lives in your root and wood.

Beneath, you hold the grave
Of him I could not save.
He was the world's angel-swarm
Himself, when he was warm,
And loss of his wise voice
Took brightness from Dyddgu's face.

He made all things grow for her,
Rich crops and clover.
Yew tree, it's your turn
To show how well you mourn.
Gently guard his tombstone,
Weep, like a maid, alone;
With your roots like a tripod
Take care you never tread
One step from his head.

And yew tree, for your care,
Goats shall not soil or tear

The house of your lord.
Fire you can discard,
And loss from carpenter
And stripping cobbler.
True love won't carve a name
On the bark of your frame,
Nor shall woodman bend
For fear of punishment
To axe through the boughs
Of my friend's green house.

Green, Dafydd, grows your roof,
Like the freshness of love.

# AT THE PUBLISHERS'
*(for Cecil Day-Lewis, 1904–1972)*


Sitting together in your office, side
by side in that comically small room,
we were so arranged, you said, because
a countryman of mine, a Welshman whose book
you were turning away with personal courtesy,
had threatened you bluntly over the face of the desk.
"I allow no man sitting in a bloody office,"
he'd shouted, "to tell me how to write poetry!"
But he was in truth the gentlest Welshman,
his violence flat as sand and quickly draining.
He became your loyal friend: of course.
And this was told to make me feel at ease.

Years later I called again, asked you to lunch,
but you couldn't come, waved at a heap of work
you had to read, the piled letters queueing
for answers. Amused, I watched you open
the world's smallest pack of sandwiches,
perhaps the size of a book of postage stamps.
Your secretary brought you a glass of water,
London water, used, and used, and used again.
Next day you were announced the new Laureate.
You knew, of course, but hadn't said a word.
No, like the swollen cancers you carried with you,
You waited for the proper day to come.

# THE GREEN BRIDGE

What shall we write about, in
Wales, where the concentration
Camps are a thousand years old,

And some of our own making?
I live in England, seem English,
Until my voice and wider

Eloquence betray me: then
I am a discovered alien.
I walk on Teifi banks, through

Snowdrops left us by the Romans,
Watching the river pour to death
In the sea, the February sea

Where Irish wailing thinly rides
The water. I have a blood group
Common only in Carmarthenshire.

The Wales I walk is a green bridge
To death — not yet, please God —
On which I am not lonely;

But journey on, thinking of
The dead Irish; hearing, far off,
The owners of Africa calling for freedom.

# BURNING THE BRACKEN

When summer stopped, and the last
Lit cloud blazed tawny cumulus
Above the hills, it was the bracken

Answered; its still crests
Contained an autumn's burning.
Then, on an afternoon of promised

Cold, true flames ripped
The ferns. Hurrying fire, low
And pale in the sun, ran

Glittering through them. As
Night fell, the brindle
Flambeaux, full of chattering

We were too far to hear, leapt
To the children's singing.
"Fire on the mountain," we

Chanted, who went to bed warmed
By joy. But I would know that fires
Die, that the cold sky holds

Uneasily the fronds and floating
Twigs of broken soot, letting
Them fall, fall now, soft

As darkness on this white page.

# MOUNTAINS POLECATS PHEASANTS

I have seen these hills closed
By impassive winter, and stood,
Banging my arms, on the last
Cold yard of road before snow
Came down on memory, the way

Strange as Asia. In summer,
Loss of the travelled sun drops
A bulk of mountain into shadow
Deep enough to lose a town in,
And scared cars, smaller, run

For the lit valleys. I thought
The mountains safe in my mind
From all revelation, but
Had never before driven late
Their cleft passes. Midnight

Had left the road as I climbed
The foothills, the car slotted
Behind headlights and the warmed
Engine humming at gradients
Above the farms. Fenceless

The ponies slept, their fetlocks
Still, their wild skulls fallen
To stone. It was a dark
Palpable as ice on those
Stone ranges. On a blunt rise,

Where the wind scorched black
The stump hawthorns and hedge
Grass bent thick in the shock
Of wind, I saw in my lights
Such tiny brilliances. Not cats',

Not foxes' eyes shone colder.
Cutting the engine, I softened

Downroad to where they were:
Polecats, the mother stiff
With instinct, her emeralds of

Sight full on my pointing;
Her five young, caught
In a lesson of hunting.
Fear moved her, sliding her
Flat as oil and under

The light; but her innocents
Stayed, weaving their baby heads.
They mewed, their sweet throats
Tame as milk. Their gentling
Cries showed me their kindling,

Blind in a hard nest under
The piled rocks. I knew the slit
Of their eyes against the thunder
Of light. I wished for them
A lenient dark and safe home.

Last year, in true daylight,
At a faultless eighty on
Other roads, it was soft
Death I passed. A bag, burst
Cushion, cracked feathers drift-

ing after smash, the hen
Pheasant lay. There was no
Terror in that sight. When
She was puffed to one side
In a bundle of snapped

Shafts, she lay roundly where
She fell. The slow blood
Failed to mark the air
For her, but in the fallen
Wreaths of her plumes ran

Her dozen chicks, no more
Than hours after hatching.
I could not catch them, nor
Could I harry them to safe
Hiding before rough

Death wiped their brief
Smudges under the wheels
Of cars. The stuff of
The roads, oil, grit, fine
Dust, absorbed their stain.

There was nothing to show for them,
Though they came from the perfect
Eggs this mother alone could form.
When she died, feathers hung
A week in the hedge, turning

Black in the hot exhausts.
I know that my polecats
Are old now in the deaths
Of their needed victims,
I know there are cold times.

When the fields whistle
In fear of them, the grass
Thickens as they ripple
Through, tearing murder. Yet
I would have had them meet,

Polecats and pheasants, on
Their common hills. I would
Have had them live, and
In a night more terrible
Than the terrible fall

Of shadow or winter over
These mountains I close again,
Let the truth turn clear
For them, the last whimper
Of it, true hunted, true hunter.

# THE THRUSH SINGING

*(from the Welsh of Dafydd ap Gwilym, fl. 1340–1370)*

Strong was the art and onrush
Of a flecked singer, the thrush
Who from the tree's height sprang
His unfettered singing.
Listen, oh let your ear fill!
No voice for the sorrowful,
But loud for the proud boy
And girl in early May
He whistles out a love-note
With every pulse of his throat.

Brook-clear, carol-call, day-bright,
Music lucid as light
He sang again and again,
Of happiness without pain,
Yesterday, all yesterday,
While I beneath a birch lay.

His reverend feathers on,
He reads the morning lesson
Exultant from his thicket:
He sets morning alight.
Hill-seer, light's interpreter,
Love's poet of leafy summer,
He sings as his privilege
Every song of the stream's edge,
Every soft, honey sonnet,
Every organ throb below it,
Spendthrift of his nature's art
To capture a girl's heart.
He preaches, bidding us come

To Ovid's flawless kingdom,
This bird, perfect priest of
May, headlong voice of love.

Lovers meet at his birch-tree
And he offers them freely
The deep wealth of his passion.
Or he'll sing where he's hidden
In a tangle of hazel —
Cloister-trees and bird-angel —
Songs lost by Heaven's fallen,
Songs he makes from love alone.

# DEERHOUND

There are no deerhounds in Wales —
Or perhaps one; in Cardiff, loping
On an elegant lead in Llandaff Fields,
Exotic in Queen Street, posing
For photographs. But there are
No true deerhounds. Our fat corgis
Sit irritably in English country houses,
Our loyal collies starve
Behind the doors of roadless farms.

We parade our terriers. Square
And bristling, the brisk wire-
haired fox terrier, the Welsh terrier
Indigenous black and tan, thin
Scars on head and legs, like a collier.
We like these dogs. I knew one
Curl herself over a drunk man's heart,
On a moor filling with blizzard.
They grin at death with their teeth.

I would have a deerhound coloured
Slippery as charcoal, running
Tactfully at the edge of eyesight,
Soft as dust after his great quarry.
Once, back of the ruined hills, I saw
A fabulous hare living on grass
Too small for sheep, thrusting,
Through coal-spoil. He leapt
In my sleep for months.

With such small deer my hound
Would not soil his slobber.
In darkness, on the edge of terror,
He would run loose, he would run loose and
Noiseless. Black as nightfur, kicking
Into the black, what antlered
Game he would rip at, what
Terrible beasts drag back
Alive for my keeping.

# MOONDAISIES

They open from a hard involucre,
Stand about two feet high, are
Rayed and arrayed in white: summer
Flowers, whitest in hot weather.

They grip the soil at hedgesides,
Opening their spotless moons above
What grass they live in. Children love
Them. They are more candid than any words.

Grow best in railway cuttings, deep
Bees among their petals, but grow
Anywhere; radiant, stubborn, cut low
By winter; common as hope.

# BEACHMASTER

His mother, from the loving sea
Lurching, found him by smell,
Though the nursery beach
Was thick with milk, and other
Blubber. Her comfort was all
Tacky liquid and the touch

Of nuzzle and rubbery flipper.
Weak and thin at first, he was
Afraid of water. But grew
Lusty, casting in plump sleep
His long, white, birthday fur.
In a ring it lay. He was

Left miniature sleek seal.
After three weeks she abandoned
Him, the call of heavy bull
In the sexual tide and swell
Being too much, though he moaned
With his pup's silk mouth the whole

Of a day. That night he snarled
At the spray and set off.
In ten weeks such a pup, in
Its first green diving of
The seaways, untaught, alone
In bottle-coloured water,

Swam six hundred miles, to Spain.
That was not my pup, though he
Savaged fast shoals in places
Far away, and dragged his growing
Awkwardly over other beaches.
This is his country, where young

Cows come out to call him home
And meadows of the sea swing

Miles deep under him. Here
He first fought, nostrils popping
In muscled water, in fury
Of instinct, for a territory.

He keeps ward off shore, armour
Of scar thickening shoulder
And neck; hulk bull, upright
In lull. Nobody sees him eat.
On the loud beach, his sons, small,
Weak, wait for white fur to fall.

# JULY THE SEVENTH

Drugged all day, the summer
Flagged in its heat, brutal
Weather sullen as brass.
There was no comfort in darkness.
Hotter than breath we lay

On beds too warm for moving,
Near open windows. Full of
Spaces the house was, walls
Fretting for a brisk air.
A door slammed flat in its

Loud frame, banging us awake.
Wind was bringing in the storm.
Quick switches of whipped light
Flicked the rooftops, made shadowless
The ends of rooms. The stopped clock

Marked the lightning. I got up
Heavily, shut the house against
Thunder. Rain was a long time
Coming, then sparse drops, stinging
Like metal, hit the bricks, the hot

Pavements. When it sweetened
To plenty, the streets tamed it,
Flowed it in pipes and conduits,
Channelled it underground through
Stony runnels. The rain brought

So faint a smell of hay I searched
My mind for it, thinking it memory.
I lay freshly awake on the cool sheets,
Hearing the storm. Somewhere, far off,
Cut grass lay in files, the hay spoiling.

# SHADOWS

## (for John Ormond)

In the night world, it was
The river was black.
Not reeds at the water's
Edge, streaked with darkness,
Not the dim coldness, back
Under the trees, were black.

It was the river. And
He lay in his smooth pool,
Slack in it, blind
In it, fanning the sand
Under him, with his tail.
He did not hear at all

Quick whispers on the bank,
Nor the furtive launching
From the brink
Of the river. His roof broke
In a small furrow along
The bend, in the swing

Of the current. He did
Not know. He lay safe
In his size, the cold
Strength that none could
Be stronger. With a flick of
His neck he could rip off

The cheap lures cast for him,
He could bull the water
Until it boiled after him,
Even out of heavy calm,
Even out of warm summer
Glaze, with his bludgeoning shoulder.

But now he lay in the balm
Tide, under the boat sailed

Secretly to kill him,
And he did not know. For him
Alone the darkness held
Its breath over river and field.

When the light slashed
The water, white torch
Pointed at him, lanced
At him, he held clenched
Against fright in the touch
Of light. He did not flinch

From lick of light, the sun
Itself in the healthy day
Did not disturb him when
He rolled in his weight down
Bending falls. But now
It was the shadow

Of his fear hung under
Him, black, ominous, pressed
Flat against gravel. Whether
The mincing river
Trembled it, or greed
Quivered the hawk boat,

He knew in his skin
The hunger of its waiting.
And he turned quietly in
From the edge of light, watching
It turn with him, cling
To him; and it ran

Behind him and under
Him as he ran
From the closing floor
Of the river.
His shadow ran
As close as the pain

Of his terror, and now
He swam furiously from
It, up, from it, away
From it, into
The clear light of freedom.
And the murderous gaff saved him.

And our faces stared red,
Reflecting
His gashed blood.
The shadow of his killing,
Sunk under mortal stain,
Waits other lights, other salmon.

# WINTER BIRDS

Most mornings now they're there,
Humped on the chestnut fence
Awaiting the regular hour
That brings me out of the shower,
Warm, pulling on my pants,
Enjoying a last yawn.
They might have been there since dawn,

And have been for all I know.
So I crumble up their bread
As a famished one or two
Hop down onto the snow —
Thrushes, all bold eye
And cream and coffee feather.
How they confront the weather!

It is habit, I suppose,
That brings these birds to wait,
And the natures that they all
So variously inherit
Show up as they strut and eat —
These starlings now, they call
Their friends to share the meal.

And when all seems to have gone
An elegant wagtail comes,
Turning his slender neck
And precise, selective beak
To feed on specks so small
They seem not there at all.
He eats the crumbs of crumbs.

But the harsh, predatory,
Scavenging, black-headed gulls
Uncertainly wheel and call,
Or balefully sit in the field.
Though fiercely hunger pulls

They will not come for the bread
And fly at the lift of my head.

But it is the gulls I hear
As I take the car down the road,
Their voices cold as winter,
Their wings grey as a cloud.
They've had nothing from my hands,
And I wish before dark fall
Some comfort for us all.

# IN OCTOBER

Moving into fall, I give my body rest
After heady summer. The hills turn early blue,
                The rivers are rising.

Yesterday, winds from the untempered north
Put me shutting windows. At night I closed my eyes
                On the last of summer.

I have set the fire, collecting the slight
Twigs. Spent as leaves, I watch my fallen hands,
                The bark hardening.

# SKULLS

Last night the snow came,
And again we face
Honest weather. The fence
That held its rose
So lightly is bent now
Under splintering snow.
It's winter. A flint cold
Has turned the house around

And the door hums in the wind.
If I went into the field,
Hearing the dry trees groan
In their barren cracking,
I would feel bones
Underfoot, winter's bones
Through snow, the furrow
Harder than the plough.

The ground's bone-hard. I first
Heard this in a place
Where snow was kindness.
Amazed, we had forced
Hard grass with our boots
Until it snapped. The clouds
Were scooped by easterlies
That set us hopping. It was

Our pink bones we imagined
Broken on that playground.
Long after a long snow,
After its memory,
When the dry had grown
Generously warm and sudden
Over as much world
As I remembered,

I went through a clarity
Of light in the early

Morning. And I climbed,
Climbed higher in the warmed
Hills than ever before.
Far away the sea
Burned, but I turned
To the last height

The growing sun could reach;
Then over it. Winter's touch
Lay there, unflawed
In a lake of snow
Below the peak. It was
A still depth, silence
For the raven's eye,
Holding its circled

Cold against the wreck
Of warmer seasons. Sprawled rock
Marked it, and a little
Moss. That world was all
Stillness; there was
No breathing in the place.
Skulls, the skulls of
Ponies, lay calmly dead above

The three-month snow, neckbones
Bent into snow, snow
Between the yellower hoops
Of their ribs. I had
Surprised them in their old
Deaths. Meek, vulnerable,
Stripped of flesh, muscle,
The last excuse of sinew,

They lay in a season
Too deep for sun,
For any weather to bother them.
Should the hornet
Perch in the empty

Pit of the eye, they
Would not startle. Let
Solid ice form

Its weight of the waterfall,
They would not huddle
Under the cliff. Their
Teeth, innocent of fear,
Were bare for birds to
Pick over. I let them lie,
The low dead in their cold,
While I caught at the comfort

Of breath. When I let fly
A wild call through
The hilly dark, momently
The birds eased from the
Ledges, croaked, then
Lofted home. Again
I called, but nothing moved.
A mountain silence filled

The rock crevices.
I think of those open skulls
When winter comes, and coldest
Air reveals us. I lace
Heavy boots, break brittle ice,
Feel winter's bones
Under the snow. I hold
My skull to the wind.

# THE TWELVE STONES OF PENTRE IFAN

The wind
Over my shoulder
Blows from the cold of time.

It has
Shaped the hill,
It has honed the rock outcrops

With the
Granules of its
Rasping. When the old ones

Were born
They dropped in dark-
ness, like sheep, and hot animals

Howled for
The afterbirths.
I watch the great stones of

Faith they
Moved in the flickering
Mountains of their nameless

Lives, and
See once more the
Points of adjusted rock, taller

Than any
Man who will ever
Stand where I stand, lifting their hope

In still,
Huge stone, pointed
To the flying wind. The sea ebbs again,

And round
The endless brevity
Of the seasons the old men's cromlech

Prepares
Its hard shadows.
The four great stones, elate and springing,

And the
Smaller stones, big
As a man, leaning in, supporting.

# ELEGY FOR DAVID BEYNON

David, we must have looked comic, sitting
there at next desks; your legs stretched
half-way down the classroom, while
my feet hung a free inch above

the floor. I remember, too, down
at The Gwynne's Field, at the side
of the little Taff, dancing with
laughing fury as you caught

effortlessly at the line-out, sliding
the ball over my head direct to
the outside-half. That was Cyril
Theophilus, who died in his quiet

so long ago that only I, perhaps,
remember he'd hold the ball one-handed
on his thin stomach as he turned
to run. Even there you were careful

to miss us with your scattering
knees as you bumped through
for yet another try. Buffeted
we were, but cheered too by our

unhurt presumption in believing
we could ever have pulled you down.
I think those children, those who died
under your arms in the crushed school,

would understand that I make this
your elegy. I know the face you had,
have walked with you enough mornings
under the fallen leaves. Theirs is

the great anonymous tragedy one word
will summarise. Aberfan, I write it
for them here, knowing we've paid to it
our shabby pence, and now it can be stored

with whatever names there are where
children end their briefest pilgrimage.
I cannot find the words for you, David. These
are too long, too many; and not enough.

# A SMALL WAR

Climbing from Merthyr through the dew of August mornings
When I was a centaur-cyclist, on the skills of wheels
I'd loop past The Storey Arms, past steaming lorries
Stopped for flasks of early tea, and fall into Breconshire.
A thin road under black Fan Frynych — which keeps its winter
Shillings long through spring — took me to the Senni valley.

That was my plenty, to rest on the narrow saddle
Looking down on the farms, letting the simple noises
Come singly up. It was there I saw a ring-ousel
Wearing the white gash of his mountains; but every
Sparrow's feather in that valley was rare, golden,
Perfect. It was an Eden fourteen miles from home.

Evan Drew, my second cousin, lived there. A long, slow man
With a brown gaze I remember him. From a hill farm
Somewhere on the slope above Heol Senni he sent his sons,
Boys a little older than I, to the Second World War.
They rode their ponies to the station, they waved
Goodbye, they circled the spitting sky above Europe.

I would not fight for Wales, the great battle-cries
Do not arouse me. I keep short boundaries holy,
Those my eyes have recognised and my heart has known
As welcome. Nor would I fight for her language. I spend
My few pence of Welsh to amuse my friends, to comment
On the weather. They carry no thought that could be mine.

It's the small wars I understand. So now that forty
People lock their gates in Senni, keeping the water out
With frailest barriers of love and anger, I'd fight for them.
Five miles of land, enough small farms to make a heaven,
Are easily trapped on the drawing-board, a decision
Of the pen drowns all. Yes, the great towns need

The humming water, yes, I have taken my rods to other
Swimming valleys and happily fished above the vanished
Fields. I know the arguments. It is a handful of earth
I will not argue with, and the slow cattle swinging weightily
Home. When I open the taps in my English bathroom
I am surprised they do not run with Breconshire blood.

# RHYDCYMERAU
*(after the Welsh of Gwenallt, 1899–1969)*


The green blades are planted to be timber for the third war,
In the earth of Esgeir-ceir and the meadows of Tir-bach,
Near Rhydcymerau.

I remember my grandmother at Esgeir-ceir,
Pleating her apron by the fire,
The skin of her face as yellow as a manuscript of Peniarth,
And the old Welsh on her lips, the Welsh of Pantycelyn.
She was part of the Puritan Wales of the last century.
I never saw my grandfather, but he was a character;
A small, quick, dancing creature –
And fond of his pint.
He had bounced straight out of the eighteenth century.
They raised nine children;
Poets, deacons, Sunday School teachers,
The natural leaders of that small community.

My uncle Dafydd, nature poet and local wit,
Used to farm Tir-bach.
His sly little song about the rooster was famous in the farms:
        "The little cockerel is scratching
            Now here, now there, about the garden."
I spent my summer holidays with him,
Watching the sheep, and making lines of cynghanedd,
Englynion and eight-line songs in seven-eight measure.
He in turn had eight children,
The first a minister with the Calvinistic Methodists,
And also a poet.
We were a nest of poets in our family.

And now there are the trees, only the trees.
Usurping roots sucking the old soil dry;
Trees, where once it was neighbourly,
An army of forest where clean pasture was,
The bastard Saxon of the south instead of poetry and scripture.
The dry cough of the fox has precedence
Over the voices of child and lamb.

And in the dark centre
Is the lair
Of the English Minotaur;
And on the trees
As on crosses
The bones of poets, deacons, preachers and teachers of Sunday School
Bleach in the sun.
And the torrent of rain washes them, they are dried by the rubbing wind.

# BRIDGES

Imagine the bridge launched, its one foot
Clamped hard on bedrock, and such grace
In its growth it resembles flying, is flight
Almost. It is not chance when they speak
Of throwing a bridge; it leaves behind a track
Of its parallel rise and fall, solid
In quarried stone, in timber, in milled
Alloy under stress. A bridge is

The path of flight. A friend, a soldier,
Built a laughable wartime bridge over
Some unknown river. In featureless night
He threw from each slid bank the images
Of his crossing, working in whispers, under
Failing lamps. As they built, braced spars,
Bolted taut the great steel plugs, he hoped
His bridge would stand in brawny daylight, complete,

The two halves miraculously knit. But
It didn't. Airily they floated above
Midstream, going nowhere, separate
Beginnings of different bridges, offering
The policies of inaction, neither coming
Nor going. His rough men cursed, sloped off,
Forded quite easily a mile lower.
It was shallow enough for his Land Rover.

I have a bridge over a stream. Four
Wooden sleepers, simple, direct. After rain,
Very slippery. I rarely cross right over,
Preferring to stand, watching the grain
On running water. I like such bridges best,
River bridges on which men always stand,
In quiet places. Unless I could have that other,
A bridge launched, hovering, wondering where to land.

# WTHAN MOONFIELDS

These are my fields in the moon's frost,
The summer coldness

Which is the night's alert while we keep abed;
And I am sleepless

Walking the dry, white meadows where,
A fortnight since,

Alun brought his scything tractor. Already
It is the newer grass

I bend with my thin slippers, already
The fragile pressures

Of my passing blacken under the moon, with
Finite shadows

Blacken. In the morning, temporary sun
Persuading us,

I'll walk warm abroad; but now I turn
Under the querulous

Owls for what comfort I can arrange
From darkness,

From summer ice. I know them well,
The Wthan moonfields.

# WATER VOICES

# CHRISTMAS DAY, 1973

Winter drought, and a parched wind
Roughens the mud. Wrapped in a parka,
Leaning bleakly into the slack
The blast misses screaming over

The blackthorn, I'm tramping a
Chalk ditch from the downs. Leaves
Dry as cornflakes crack under
My gum-boots, the hedge is against

My shoulder. Sands of their flying
Dusts hunt the spent fields, ice
Grains stick at my eyes. Caught
On the thorns, a rip of news-print

Shivers its yellow edges, grows
Long, then rises easily, a narrow
Heron, out of shadow. It rises,
Trailing its thin legs, into cold

Sun flat as the land. Upright,
Broad wings spread, neck curved
And head and great blade turned
Down on the lit breast, it hangs

Against barbs, against winter
Darkness, before its slow vanes
Beat once over the elms, a
Christ crucified, a flying Christ.

# LEAR AT FIFTY

This morning early, driving the lanes in my
  Glib metal, frost fur on the brambles,
The grass, the hasps and bars of gates, first
  Sun burning it away in clinging wisps,
I saw an old man, sweeping leaves together, outside
  The Black Horse. His face held night's

Stupor, the lines of his age had not stiffened
  Against the daylight. He shifted his
Feet to careful standing, and then his broom,
  His necessary crutch, moved like an
Insect on slow, frail, crawling legs from
  Leaf to leaf. The small gusts of

My passing broke his labour, heaps of the dry
  Work spilling and flying. Nobody
Walked on the shore. Waves, unexpected heavy waves
  From some wild, piling storm away at sea,
Ripped the mild sand, smashed rocks, and shot the
  Squalling gulls out of the filth, vomit

And glittering sewage the flung birds flocked for.
  And truly, the tide was high this morning:
Old shoes, cans, cynical gouts of accidental oil,
  Plastic bottles, ropes, bubbling detergent
Slime, all were thrown to the sea-wall. I have
  No wish to remember those unwelcoming

Waves I turned my back on, nor to think of old men
  Sitting tight in their skulls, aghast
At what their soft, insistent mouths will keep on
  Yelling. But through the limpet hours
I've walked the fields as if on a cliff's edge,
  The idea of flight in me, and seen my

Friends, myself, all strong, governing men, turned
   Sticks, turned tottering old fools.
The last sun in its blaze brings yellow light
   To everything, walls, windows, water;
A false warmth. In the morning some old man will start
   To sweep his leaves to a neatness.

# I.M. JAMES CHUANG, M.B., B.S., M.R.C.S., R.N., DIED APRIL 23, 1978, AGED 25

Last Thursday morning, watching a haul of barges
tug their blunt ropes under Chelsea Bridge,
I saw two swallows, hot from Africa,
flick and scream across the delighted river.
First of the warming year, emblem and omen,
one for each day of all that remained of your life.

Jim, I can't understand how anyone as young
and generous could go so swiftly into death.
It was good that afternoon, walking in Hyde Park,
watching the little goldeneye, pair by pair
in meticulous black and white, bobbing
On the cold Serpentine. To see them dive!

They'd slip under the water so casually,
without taking breath, without preparation
slide into the silence, longer and deeper
until we couldn't see them. They all came back.
One by one all popped up from their underworld,
out of their darkness. Small London children,

playing with grandparents, clapped their hands
at each abrupt return. We spoke of your work
at Greenwich Hospital, the Seamen's Hospital
down by the widening Thames, and I was startled
by the wholeness of your compassion, your serious
tolerance. You were a chosen man. Somewhere

away from my awareness you had come of age.
And since then I've been finding it difficult
to remember you as a small boy, that brush-head,
the apricot-coloured child who would bring his

reading book, or the older one in Christ's
Hospital blue, alert, eager, always smiling.

On Thursday afternoon I knew you the full man,
conscious of healing, able to keep death at bay
down there near the river. Images of your childhood
were not wanted. You had become my contemporary,
although you were young enough to clap your hands
with the children, and I stand in an older body.

(Conscious of certain wreck, Jim, I had meant
to ask about arthritis, how my fingers stiffen;
but had not thought to know the pain of knocking
these words out.) To think a starling's nest,
untidy tangle of instinct pressed messily
into an air vent, could have killed you.

Anger meant little to you  If I am angry
it is a futility you must allow me now,
Two Canada geese, those heavy winter birds,
grey on a grey sky, beat overhead, trailing
silence behind their ponderous flying.
A cold evening has come back to the country.

# PONIES

Stepping delicately, the ponies, the palominos,
Yellower than cream, smooth as butter, as bright
As the swags of ragwort they step among.

Stones in the river Brân, rounded as bubbles,
Limestone and sandstone tumbled from Fwng and Cedny,
And brilliant shallow water over them.

Heavy over the viaduct the belligerent engine,
Imminent, cloudless thunder beneath the arches,
A young man's tombstone under the hollow echo.

> *A white rose, his quiet life*
> *Fell in quiet to his grave.*
> *Quiet now, without a breeze,*
> *He sleeps in quiet, sleeps in peace.*

Unmoving, in an old darkness near the river,
The inquisitive ponies, the mild palominos,
Standing among hawthorns, snags of wild roses.

]

# LINES FOR THE BASTARD PRINCE

His father's empty coffin, chipped
from the stone with a driven chisel
to keep the old man cold. Here spread
his hollow shoulders, and there

his ankle-bones were clipped. The air
and powder of those flying bones are lost.
But the boy's different. A blunt middle-weight,
balanced, powerful, such energy's even about

his rest his effigy can scarcely hold him in.
Oh, he was a tough one, neat and brutal
in attack, with a fast counter. His mother
was a fresh girl from the villages, her

blood could not expect the honour
of a cut tomb in the chapel, she did not
earn for her feet a carved dog, symbol
of fidelity. This firm prince is her memorial.

# AT THE SEA'S EDGE, IN PEMBROKESHIRE

Peter de Leia, dead eight
hundred years, began this
structure. Not having the
saint's art, nor learned
his psalter from a gold–
beaked pigeon, he built
in common stone. He exalted
labour into a stone praise.

Nor was he baptised in live
waters conveniently burst
forth to supply the shaken
drops for that ceremony. To
reach his pulpit he climbed
a joiner's steps, did not expect
the ground to lift in a sudden
hillock so that he could preach
in open piety to the rapt Welsh.

When he laid down the square-
ended presbytery, with aisles,
transepts, tower and nave, he saw
his masons bleed if the chisel
slipped. One fell in his sight
from the brittle scaffolding
and the two legs snapped
audibly, hitting the ground.
He had not the saint's skill

to stop that falling which must
fall. Such clear faith was not
possible, the rule of the world
grown strong. He knew that right
building was a moral force, that
stone can grow. An earthquake
has tested this cathedral. In

Pembrokeshire, near the saint's
river, at the edge of the sea,

de Leia built well, saw stone
vault and flower. A plain man,
building in faith where God
had touched the saint, he saw
the miracle which is not swift
visitation, nor an incredible
suspension of the commonplace,
but the church grown great about us,
as if the first stone were a seed.

# UNCHANGING

Every seven years, is it, the body's
Changed? Flake by dry flake the skin
Renewed, glands and muscles altered
Secretly in their smooth liquids?
Hair, nails, how we shear them away,
Slow modifications unnoticed almost,
Until one day an accident of the mirror
Shows the remade man, grown different

Silently. All's changed then; eyes,
Manipulation of the senses, the very
Instruments of love are changed. The world's
Grown calcinous. What miracle, when
That which we call the heart is still
Immutable constancy, unchanged love.

## MOONMAN

Last night I walked under the moon,
One of its green shadows, my eyes
A reflection of the chill moon.

Rounder than harvest, more cold
Than remembered frost, it burned
With sterile ardour the skin

Of the lane I walked. I know
It will be diminished, pared
Crescent recognisably, but say

It must grow again in its due time
More coldly blazing for the sleek
Ice to come. I had not thought

How I, too, wane as you turn away
Your sunlight, am great only
In harvests of your love.

# CAVE PAINTINGS

### i. *After Dark*

After dark, police sirens rip us
Awake. We crouch, hands over ears, our walls
Too small to hold such raucous invasion.

In Woodland Park, in caves
Of municipal concrete, the wolf
Shivers, the cougar shakes her chained ears.

### ii. *A Dish of Pebbles*

Pebbles in a dish: opal, jade,
And one against sufficient light
A palpable smoke. All these

Are from California beaches. But here's
From Oregon a stone, from the castellated
Rim of the continent, its moats holding

Sea-lions, voices of moist caves. Spray
Decorates the sky, the rattle of draining
Pebbles runs south from river-mouth to river-

Mouth. Here are sharks' teeth, two, for
Needling, blood-letting. And I have arrowheads:
This, from Washington; that, of greater age, from Somerset.

### iii. *A Thrush*

The thrush comes into the house, I hear
Its soft battering against the window-glass.

And I leave my desk, speaking to it,
Tolerate its panic, its round, wild eye,

The way it spreads its wings in a bare
Ache against the pane. I am accustomed

To creatures, release it. It leaves behind
Two slight feathers, the yellow stain of its droppings.


*iv. Ancestor*

There is no photograph, but I think him
Tall. He stood in twenty acres of grass
And a whole unfenced mountain uprose

Behind him. Certainly he worked
Eight sons timid, ruled all daylight,
Roaring at animals. Left, at the end,

Nothing, but was the last of us, long
Ago, to come off that brutal soil with
Innocent power. So I think him tall.


*v. In Still Clay*

A Staffordshire greyhound, fawn, couchant,
Thin, stylised neck and flexible white hocks,
He sits in still clay on a dais of royal blue.

Six inches in length, the glaze crazed
Nowhere, and one gold line untarnished
Along the hollow plinth, he is preserved

By lucky accident. Pharaohs knew his like.
He dreams in the shadow between two shelves,
Linking time with time. Is a potent hunter.


*vi. Scatterings of Light*

Waterfalls, pools, streams, rivers,
And the loud, monotonous, empty

[ 93 ]

Drop through the centuries; the cave
Remembers water, was drilled

By water. Scatterings
Of light floated among bats

Pendulous as fruit in the rock's
Cold branches. A dry cave holds

Darkness to its walls, as water
Holds the shape of its flowing.


## vii. Paperweight

This domed, heavy glass, it satisfies
The hand. Its concentric flowers, whorls,

Shells and coloured rods, its airy
Bubbles even, all are held in a still

Dance. I keep it for its solid
Roundness against time, and for the men,

In France two hundred years ago, who by
Some perfect means of their mortality

Made it, full and heavy, from fragile silicas,
And sent its casual permanence to my hand.


## viii. Symbols

Emblems, plaques, icons, symbols
Of the decaying hand; stones, or

Feathers, identified by warm
Sight, and touched, and put

Aside; or voices,
Transferred as they vanish

In handled syllables, we keep
From the breaking dust, against

The filling of the cave. For
The cave is filling, fills

Rapidly. It closes,
From the eyes in.

# HYPERION

was hardly a Titan. He stood
a brief inch over six feet, was
sweetly made. Not for his size
am I sent in his just praise
along the measured tracks

of his achievement. Dropped
on the printed turf by Selene,
daughter of Serenissima, he moved
even in his first uncertainty
like one waited for. His birth

was in green April, and he grew
in light, on the fat meadows.
Gently schooled, he delighted
his mentors with his perfect ardour,
honesty, the speed of his response.

Though small, he was quite beautiful,
his chestnut mane burning, his step
luminous. Some doubted his courage,
looking askance at the delicacy
of his white feet, ignoring the star

already brilliant in his forehead.
His heart was a vivid instrument
drumming for victory, loin and muscle
could stretch and flex in eating
leaps. When he ran, when he ran

the rings of his nostrils were scarlet,
the white foam spun away from his lips.
For his was the old, true blood,
untainted in his veins' walls:
two lines to St. Simon, two lines

to Bend Or: The Flying Dutchman,
Bayardo, Galopin, all the great ones
back in his pedigree met in him.
He could not fail to honour
his fathers in the proud flood

of his winning. Nine times he left
his crescent grooves in the cheering
grass before the commoners gasped
after him. At Epsom, racing as if
alone on the classic track, he won

a record Derby, at Doncaster the Leger.
He won the Chester Vase, the Prince
of Wales's Stakes. Nor in his fullness,
drowsing in quiet fields in quiet company,
was he forgotten. His children,

sons and daughters of the Sun,
did not allow this. Hypericum,
Sun Chariot, Rising Light, all
were his. And Sun Stream, Midas.
Owen Tudor, Suncastle, many others.

The swift Godiva was his, and in
his image famous Citation, who ran
away with all America. Sportsmen,
all who go to the races, who marvel
at the flying hooves, remember Hyperion.

# ORMONDE

The great Ormonde was a roarer —
unsound in wind: but was never beaten.

The loud blemish of his flesh
suggests mortality, that he was

to be reached by some pretender.
It was a deceitful flaw. The horse

was perfect. Winning the Guineas,
"he took despotic command, sped

forward, galloped over everything,
won cantering." So John Porter

of Kingsclere, his trainer, exulting.
Carrying unjust weight, he was ridden,

by Archer often, to extravagant wins
in great events, was led in his fame

over the Thames to Park Lane, where all,
at their champagne, were delighted

by his charm, his grave manners. He ate
his sugar from ladies' gloved fingers

and went amiably home. After which
the ingrate Duke of Westminster sold him;

sold to the Argentine his greatness, the
one Ormonde. His few offspring never

lived up to him. How could they,
measured against perfection, do other

than disappoint? Even in age, tendons
inflexible as bone, blunt clubs

too far from his thinning blood to sense
the turf, he would not be defeated.

I have to think that natural death
stood off in awe and would not take

the match on level terms. A bullet
killed him, smacking into his skull

before the old horse truly knew
he was under orders. As well he was

unprepared. He would have outrun death.

# GROOMING

The poem stands on its firm
legs. Its claws are filed, brush
and curry-comb have worked
with the hissing groom to polish

its smooth pelt. All morning, hair
by hair, I've plucked away each small
excess; remains no trace of
barbering, and all feels natural.

It is conditioned to walk, turn
to the frailest leash, swing
without effort into ecstatic
hunting. Now I am cleaning

the teeth in its lion jaws
with an old brush. I'll set it
wild on the running street, aimed
at the hamstring, the soft throat.

## THE BEAUTIFUL YOUNG
## DEVON SHORTHORN BULL
## SEXTON HYADES XXXIII

In warm meadows this bull
Ripens, gently. He is a pod
Of milky seed, not ready yet.
Not liking to be alone, he
Drifts on neat feet to be near
His herd, is sad at gates
When one is taken from him. There's
No red in his eye, he does not
Know he's strong, but mildly

Pushes down hedges, can carry
A fence unnoticed on his broad
Skull. His flat back measures
The horizon. Get a ladder, look
Over him. Dream that, one by one,
The far fields fill with his children, his soft daughters.

# EAGLE AND HUMMINGBIRD

Demure water, soft summer water,
Its rolling boulders dropped, its carried logs
Cast white as salt upon some resting beach,
I throw my spinners here, those small, beaked suns
Turning through steelheads, cutthroat, and the
Five-pound salmon come from the sea too young
Along the green channel of their instinct.

I stand midstream on rock, its roots in water,
Using the air to fly my singing line,
The burning spindle drifting through the river,
The river alders burning in the sun;
United elements, the one forgiving world
In whose veined heart I stand in a blue morning
Beneath the flash of hummingbirds, the smoulder

Of fishing eagles. Water and sun, fire
And reflected fire, the hundred suns
The river's mirror carries under the trees,
Buoyancy of the light birds, all's here,
All, all is here. And my thin line holds now
The lure of the hummingbird, its spinning
Breast, and the hooked voice of the eagle.

# RAVENNA BRIDGE

Thinking he walked on air, he
Thrust each step, stretched straight
His ankle. We saw him lift
On thinnest stone between him-
self and earth, and then dip on.

Such undulant progress! Stern
Herons walk like that; but he
Just rose again into his
Highest possible smiling air,
Stepped seriously by us,

And kept for all himself
The edges, even, of his happiness.
Passing, we caught the recognition
Of his transfiguring sweet
Smoke. And so he stepped, he

Skipped, the thin boy, on narrow
Ravenna Bridge, itself a height
Over pines and sycamores. He
Danced above their heads. If
He'd hopped the hand-rail, had

Swayed into flight, fallen
To stony death among wood-doves,
We should have watched him. I did
Not stand as I felt, hand
To mouth in a still gasp, but

Coldly and relaxed, and saw the boy
Perform his happy legs across
Ravenna Bridge and up the hill
To Fifty-second. We walked home,
Thanking his god, and ours.

# A READING IN SEATTLE

Cold snow covers the summer
Mountains; they do not reject it.
Seas towed from Asia, immense
Pacific waters, invade the bays,
Roll heavy the long coast, turn
With a shake of the spray
And splinter the bleached
Lumber, sieve the lion-
coloured sand. Inland, with
Lakes and the tamed
Salt of the Sound, is the lovely
City, safe in its washed air,
Holding its bridges calmly,
Its trees and tended grass,
The welcome of its wooden
Houses. At night, many
Lamps glitter cleanly, form
Stars in reflecting water
By skittering winds disturbed,
By small boats softly home
From fishing. The people sleep
In a ring of Japanese hills.
A hundred miles away a cone-
shaped mountain measures the light.

Rivers, the rivers too.
Drop by plain drop they fall
From the cracking glaciers,
Collect in forming channels,
Roar, released, torrent of jade,
Opalescent fluid jewel,
Route of the salmon's instinct.
I stood once at the Skagit's edge
On a hot day, my face burned,
And walked slowly in, one step,
And another step, until I was
Waist-deep in green flowing,

One with it, with the water.
Driving away through the little
Homesteads I was bereft. No man
Stands twice in the same river.

In the evening I thought
Of Dylan, how he had read
In Seattle. "The little slob,"
My friend said, marvelling,
"He read Eliot so beautifully,
Jesus, I cried." I did not answer.
In the city now the bars are
Empty of his stories
And only the downtown Indians
Are drunk as his memory.

I read in a hall full
Of friends, students, serious
Listeners. The great dead
Had spoken there, Auden,
Roethke, Watkins, many others.
There was room for a plump ghost.
I thought I heard his voice
Everywhere, after twenty years
Of famous death. The party over,
I walked home, saw on peaks
The coldest snow, white as bone.

# MARYMERE FALLS

At the lip of the falls, small
Ferns totter in green air, tilt,
Lodge in a light pushed sideways,
As water, its level lost, pauses,

Grows heavy, and throws its slow
Roar outward, and down. Spray
Frets the marginal fall, imprisons
Sunlight in thin screens, climbs,

So frail its grains, against
All reasonable falling. But
Arc's full centre, its glistening
Plummet, profoundly falls, and falls

In booming pools, scatters,
Claps its steady diving over
Running stones, its words the poem's
Words: splash, rainbow, thunder.

# BELONGING

He came after the reading, when all
Had left, the students, the kind
Congratulating friends, and I was tired.

What it was gave me more than a
Public courtesy for this old man,
Small, neat in his blue suit, someone's

Grandfather, I can't say. He held
A paper faded as his eyes; his family
Tree. Anxious, erect, expecting my

Approval, he stood in the hot room.
"I'm Welsh," he said. I read his
Pedigree. Bentley, Lawrence, Faulkner,

Graydon, no Welsh names. I nodded,
Gave back his folded pride, shook
My head in serious admiration. Belonging,

After all, is mostly matter of belief.
"I should have known you anywhere," I said,
"For a Welshman." He put away his chart,

Shook hands, walked into the foreign light.
I watched him go. Outside, the sprinklers,
Waving their spraying rainbows, kept America green.

# ISLANDS OFF MAINE
*(for Charles and Jeannie Wadsworth)*

## 1.

One man hammering
From his home on crevices
Shatters the darkness
Over the islands.

Dawn moves briskly
Among the rugosas
And the harbour lights take back
Their shaken images.

Water smooth as claws
Holds its silent traps;
On the visible tide
Floats huge America.

## 2.

In the spring of the year eight ospreys
Flew over the island; smaller birds
Squalled at them, pollack and mackerel
Spun in their flustered shoals beneath

The sea-hawks' wings. Six flew on
To cull more northern waters; two stayed,
Perched much on trees, and hunted
Entirely in flight, circling. Hung

Two hundred feet above what fish
They chose; and fell, the vertical
Steep plunge between their own
Talons, then the consummate grab.

For surface fish they disturbed
No more than the sea's lace before
Flicking away water and taking off,
But can dive a yard into the packed

Ocean, feet braced thick against impact,
The toes lined with spicules, the claws
Stiff, and the whole battered water suddenly
Over their five-foot wings. They close

Their nostrils against the salt entry
And never fail. A sodden flap off
The surface they shiver away droplets,
Carry their fish head first, a torpedo.

All summer we saw their young in the
Flattened spruce top, all day we heard
Their mewling hunger, until they flew
On the cooling air, down the long coast.


3.

And on the point one day,
Mist flattening the island,
I met the mad boy.

Brambles had torn his jeans,
His fingers were harsh as carrots,
Waterbeads dropped in his bull's curls.

His voice would not behave,
His skull was echoing and
The mist was behind his eyes.

"What d'you like about Maine,
Hey, what d'you like about it?"
Screaming like a blue jay.

Mountains, I told him, mostly
The mountains, but the sea too.
His joy was terrible, he hopped

In the gritty pebbles, he slapped
His laughing over the vague beach.
"Sure, there were mountains Monday

— today there ain't mountains!"
The island stopped where he pointed,
His hand wiped out Mount Cadillac.

"When you leaving, why don't you?
Why don't you leave? If you knew
The people here, you'd leave today!"

He moved away, was a stone, a
Post, a shape among shifting
Shapes, a slow uncertainty.

Unseen gulls jeered from the rocks.
Pewter light off the water
Faded when I hit the dirt path.


4.

Pink Harding, born on the island,
Counts time in decades. Her chair
Rocks away anything smaller.

In all her years the sea has not stopped
Running. Each tide piles higher the granite
Pebbles, the red granite and the grey.

Hummingbirds visit her white phlox.
She is glad to hear this, but has seen
Them before. She is up since dawn.

We shout down her deafness, but scar tissue
Rubs at her eyes. She no longer braids
The tied rugs for which she's famous.

"Some I had ten dollars for!" she still
Marvels, "And not always the best ones."
They're heirlooms now, hang in museums.

She speaks of her father, that good man,
Then sits up, lifts one hand in pride,
"My grandfather was a full-blooded Englishman."


5.

Four white posts and a length of chain
Enclose the burial ground. Its stillness
Is twelve low headstones among the spruce.
You could walk past it, your head down

Against mosquitoes, and not see it.
Here lie the old, in the amplitude
And honour of their longevity: Capt.
Thos. Manchester, AE 92 yrs 3 mos;

Hannah, his Wife, AE 87 yrs 5 mos;
And nine others. But Gilman U. Stanley,
A boy, he sailed east and north
Out of Cranberry, past Nova Scotia,

In the temperate summer of 1861, watched
With his living eyes the Atlantic
Shake back the pack ice off Cape Breton.
All his life he'd seen harbour porpoise,

But now he called the finback whale,
The humpback whale, the minke and right
Whales as they rolled and mountained in their
Buoyant schools across the Cabot Strait.

Rich waters! O rich, destructive waters!
Working northward, never far from landfall,
They kept Anticosti to larboard, and Cape Whittle
And Little Mecatina Island; and saw on the right

The grave Newfoundland headlands where they
Should be, reaching on June 16 the Strait
Of Belle Isle. There the boy at once went
Down. The sea took him, pressed flat

His agile breath, swam him among rocks
In water blue as ice, broke him in deep
Currents so that he lolled boneless.
Son of Jonathan R. and Irene Stanley,

AE 16 yrs 8 mos 28 dys. Each year the scrub,
The quiet moss, the little evergreens, move
Like a slow green tide on his empty grave,
Break on his headstone, and the other headstones.


6.

water bell
        sea's angelus
                anchored edge of rock
and steep of water

        toll for us

audible hanging wave
        simple element
                mouth of the round tide
storm's voice

        toll for us
        in our leaving

water tongue
        clapper and safe hammer
                sea's elegy and sound

        celebrate our passing

        toll for us

# IN MAINE, SEPTEMBER

Soon now, storm windows
Will shutter the island houses.
The hummingbirds are flown,
The summer people travel south
Toward their warming dollars.
Pretty little sailboats,
Bouncing on trolleys,
Move into sheltered winters.

Its silvered bleaching
Adrift on summer grasses
And a tide of dandelions,
An old boat lies in quiet
Behind the long point.
Is an exhausted animal,
Its lines the whale's lines,
For bludgeoning, for cutting water.

# TRAVELLING WEST

March ends, and the wild month
Batters its last hours against the house.
Such driven rain, such a wind
Bellowing out of the west
Against the walls!
I sit in the late room,
Watch the curtains shiver, and think
Of the drenched counties of England,
Their shuddering pastures, the creaking fibres
Of oak and hanging beech.

The gutters are full, the uneasy road's
Awash; dazed cars buffet the flood
Behind their swimming headlights.
Perhaps the grey sea from the west
Has broken in at last, bringing
Its ancient flotsam, news
From the drowned islands, voices,
Branches of legendary trees.
But that old, distant coast
Will hold, it will hold always.

Although I saw it when the year
Had barely turned from summer,
The sea was snarling early,
Spun me as I swam, thrashed me
Among its grains with its upper hand,
Sank me in little storms.
Fighting for land, gasping,
Reeling, beaten deaf, I saw
The small farms in the hills
Light up their steady lamps.

Flew west over a sea spotted
With cloud, and three days later
Swam in kindlier water,

In Branch Lake, by the Penobscot River.
Had gone for togue and landlocked salmon,
But the sun lulled my hooks. I hung
In a hammock of water, warm silt
Soft to the toes. Mallard
Feathered above my comfort, the long
Westering light streamed through the red oaks.

I have walked hard Pacific beaches,
Skin burned raw by an insidious sun,
Stared through high arcs of spray
At seas running with tuna and oyster shell;
A man at the world's edge facing westward,
Aware that every tide is for departures;
And came home, a small Odysseus,
Having, as best I could, followed the sun.
I sit alert in the still room, hearing
The storm, knowing no end to the journey.

The chalk downs hold these rains
Like a sponge, releasing them
Through the villages in clear bournes.
Salad cresses grow there, and tiny fish,
Their world a yard of shallow pool,
Flicker among the thready roots.
The flood will be absorbed and turned
To mild uses. Five hours will bring
The sun up. We'll begin once more,
Travelling west, travelling west!

# NEW POEMS

## BERRIES

For the first time this year, berries
light up the garden. Stumbling downstairs,

grumbling, stubbing my sight against
a darkness I'm not ready for, I reach

for a switch, pause. In the garden
berries are incandescent. Frost

has uncovered the branches. Ignited fruit,
cotoneaster, holly, plump heps of damask,

of rosa rugosa, of the dry old noisette
nailed to the cold wall, all are blazing.

I stare in my dim awareness of autumn
passing, imagine how all over England

these sparks are lighting the winter;
round crab, the seeds of spindle

and wayfarer, clusters of buttery haw,
the waxy barberry, the black lamps

of ivy, beads of neglected briar,
of alder buckthorn, succulent

candles of yew. Perched on a chair,
I relish berries, warmed by their fatness.

# EARTH

Hail rattles the garden.
It scatters like white shot and
    The stung earth winces.

In summer I longed for
A cold wind. Now my neck aches
    At the first of winter.

Too late, too late!
The apple-blossom is blown and
    The sweet fruit gathered.

Like fish-scales the shine
On village roofs. The house prepares
    To reject winter.

As the leaves fall, so
The clouds multiply; it's all
    Balance, equilibrium.

Flints in the turned field,
The city's gutters, all things cry
    Endure, endure!

Dust in June, the field's
Stiff clay now; its puddles mirror
    The sullen weather.

When I was younger
I ignored dust; now I move near it,
    I watch it with love.

Is that the nestling
Which was featherless in May?
    He's hard-eyed now.

This morning the children
Raced to school. Who are these dotards
     Filling the schoolyard?

     "Consider this leaf,
Old now, dry as an egg-shell;
     It was born last April."

     As I grow older
I begin to feel how strong
     The pull of gravity.

     Turning in heaven
The pied earth; its cities move
     Into daylight, darkness.